SHARING LOVE SERIES 2016

James Edward Hyler II

ISBN: 1532781830
ISBN 13: 9781532781834

May 4th, 2016

Happy Birthday Angel Haiku

Birthday Girl Angel
You will turn 20 today
These poems are your gift

ONE IN A HUNDRED

A young sheep among a flock wandered
and as he looked around he pondered
the grass is much greener over there
I'll go yonder and not even have to share

looking and thinking the Shepherd was turned another way
the young sheep bolted and ran toward the field far away
as he ran, he thought with glee
I'm free I'm free I'm free

upon reaching the field of green grass
the young sheep began to eat very fast
without any cares and unseeing eyes
he didn't notice as a pack of wolves ascended over the rise

as the wolves ran, drawing nearer to their prey
the young sheep looked up and saw them to his dismay
he started to run frantically, looking for the flock
and seeing no one, almost went into a state of shock

running and looking frantically about
he saw by the fields edge, the woods, and let out a shout

I'll run into the woods, it will be safe
I'll get away from the wolves before it's too late

without even giving it a second thought
the young sheep entered the woods, not finding the safety he sought
the light grew from bright to dim
he could barely see in front of him

deeper into the woods he was engulfed into a fog
then he stumbled and ran into a vast bog
finally he stopped, barely able to stand
not realizing he was in quicksand

As he listened for the wolves, he heard them howl
and distantly heard as they growled
oh foolish sheep who's wandered astray
the bog will have you for it's meal today

a cold chill ran down his spine
as the young sheep tried to run to make up time
but he could not move, the quicksand held him fast
and as he sank, he knew his next breath would be his last

the last thing the sheep heard was the wolves as they laughed
not even feeling the crook of the Shepherd's staff
as he hooked it around the young sheep's neck
and pulled him from death's sandy wreck

with big, loving, and caring hands
the Shepherd nourished the sheep to life again
the young sheep rejoined the flock he once had fled
never forgetting without the Shepherd, he would be dead

EARTHWORM FLIES

The rain came down
Saturating the ground
The earthworm came up
To swim in the muck

The dove came down
Hearing a splashy splash sound
Now the earthworm flies

SHARING LOVES FIRST LIE

Sharing love Saturday night
unaware what lay in sight
self love arrived on scene
angry, drunk, stumbling, mean

sharing love stop play
sharing love on couch
we are going to talk
sharing love thought oh ouch

you told my angel to shut up
I didn't sharing love replies
you dug your hole deeper
I wont tolerate lies

I didn't sharing love cries
you did self love steams
I didn't sharing love cries
you did self love screams

I didn't sharing love pleads
you did self love proves

striking oft sharing loves face
face marked with 12 bruises

I did sharing love whispered
12 bruises now blistered
I told angel to shut up
Sharing Loves First Lie

you told the truth
I will ring angel
you apologize to atone
sharing love felt so alone

Self love dialed 777-7777
phone began to ring
angel began to sing
hello, may I help you

self love hands over phone
sharing love is sobbing
little lips moaning
I told you to shut up

what's this all about
put self love on phone
sharing love obeyed
not feeling alone

sharing love told you to shut up
told me a lie
I struck with hand
now will grow spirit of truth not lie

angel angry
began to shout
sharing love never told me to shut up
sharing love felt joy, the truth coyly out

5:00 P.M. DEATH TRAP

Finish work at 5:00 p.m.
stop at death trap
cancer sticks sold
liver killers sold
get poor quick tickets sold
doctors make more gold
patients shoveled under 6 feet of coal
human life cycle fortune cookie told

DEATH'S LIFE CYCLE

Clear blue skies
white clouds roll in
white clouds plaster sky
white clouds get black underbellies

rain sprinkles
thunder rumbles
lightening seen in distance
rain torrents

thunder sounds
lightening on horizon
thunder cannon balls
lightening sparks

forest trees to tall massive torches
trees to stubble
blackened earth remains

wild flower blooms
feeds honey bees
feeds hungry feeders

grass emerges
feeds deer
feeds hungry feeders

ALLPOETRY.COM POEM BAIT

Poem published on Allpoetry.com
gently floats to bottom of changing sea
tasted and eaten by hungering fish

until it reaches
bottom of ocean floor
finally devoured and is no more
by destructive clock demon worms

FORBIDDEN LUST TASTED

Apple dew
slowly drips
into wakening mouth

Skin of apple
peeled slowly apart
exposing living flesh

Stomach filled and engorged
fresh seeds explode into wet, hot crack
green sprouts quickly are coming back

LIGHTNING LOVE BLAST

C
creative nature
R
recycling nature
E
energy nature
M
maturing nature
A
active nature
T
thriving nature
I
invigorating nature
O
omnipresent nature
N
nature re-birth

LUST COMES IN 3'S

Swish
swish
swish
the hard broomstick blows

swoosh
swoosh
swoosh
the racing heartbeat blows

smile
smile
smile
the sweet virgin blows

FLY TEASE

U landed on my arm
i swiped at you and missed
u landed on my groin
i swiped at you and hit

i threw you on the table
u lay stunned on your back
i motioned to kill you
u retracted my actions back

u flipped on your belly
i was happy you were still alive
u flew off into the sky
i saw wings fluttering good-bye

FLY TEASE 2

I landed on your arm
u swiped at me and missed
i landed on your groin
u swiped at me and hit

u threw me on the table
i lay stunned on my back
u motioned to kill me
i retracted your actions back

i flipped on my belly
u smiled that i was still alive
i flew off into the sky
u saw my wings fluttering good-bye

TRAGIC 18 DROPS

18 water faucet drops
of remembrance
flood my brain
cascading off my tongue
as waterfalls of
18 demons

to stop the
18 water faucet drops
is to find the source
why dad? Why dad?
Did you treat me that way at
18

18 water faucet drops
of remembrance
flood my brain
cascading off my tongue
as waterfalls of
18 angels

smile dad, smile dad
you ain't treating me
like your dad treated you at
18

18 water faucet drops
turned off

SHRINKING MUD PUDDLE!

Shrinking mud puddle!
hrinking mud puddle!
rinking mud puddle!
inking mud puddle!
nking mud puddle!
king mud puddle!
ing mud puddle!
ng mud puddle!
g mud puddle!
mud puddle!
ud puddle!
d puddle!
puddle!
uddle!
ddle!
dle!
le!
e!
!

TABOO TOUCH

Windy breeze
moved sexy tan leaves
exposing tight knothole crack
on pretty brown bark back

sap started rising
and branch stiffened
as windy breeze
brushed branch into tight knothole crack

sap exploded
oozing down loose knothole crack
running down pretty brown bark back
eaten by ants in the outback

GROWING MUD PUDDLE!

g
gr
gro
grow
growi
growin
growing
growing m
growing mu
growing mud
growing mud p
growing mud pu
growing mud pud
growing mud pudd
growing mud puddl
growing mud puddle
growing mud puddle!

CHICKEN CORN CONTROL

Man eats chicken
chicken eats corn
that man planted
man 6ft planted
50 years from time born

man eats corn
that man planted
chicken as pet
man 6ft planted
100 from time born

MOTHER EARTH SEX

Mother earth mates with father seed
father seed produces maize
maize feeds eaters
eaters become eaten
re-planted in mother earth
father seed re-birth

BIRD FEEDER

I feed the birds

they eat the seed
their droppings
fall to mother earth

enriching the soil
that tree roots
eat and grow

producing leaves
releasing oxygen
I breath to live

Birds feed me

OXYGEN CEO

I'm on oxygen
breathing through tubes
in my nose

my breathe of labored pain
is CEO's breathe of green-back gain

APPLE PILL BILL

Grandmother's free advise:
an apple a day
keeps the doctor away
long life to stay

Doctor's prescription advise:
an apple pill a day
side effects dismay
the apple bill on the way

HOOTER OWL SEDUCTION

Seductive hooter owl

big blue water drop eyes
long tan slim legs
silky swishing swaying breast feathers
short perky pouty beak

ravages tiny virgin brown mouse
caught in sharp pointed tainted claws
eaten seductively and slowly with
short perky pouty beak

painted blood rose red
short perky pouty beak

MIRROR MIRROR ON THE WALL

U look at me
smile
new mirror

u look at me
frown
old mirror

u look at me
vampire
only mirror

FAITHFUL FAIR WEATHER FRIENDS

Slow sleek sailing
floating fishing boat

casually cast cheerful chum
over board

dancing diamond delicate dolphins
eat
casually cast cheerful chum

follows faithful friend
floating fishing boat

faithful fair weather friends
until we meet again

CALL ME ISHMAEL

I peg leg
smell a whale
white and pale

i peg leg
see a whale
white and pale

i peg leg
harpoon a whale
white and pale

i white whale
kill peg leg
white and pale

I THINK THEREFORE I AM

Thought
hungry
eat

thought
tired
sleep

thought
thirsty
drink

thought
angry
fight

thought
lust
sex

thought
love
kiss

thought
sad
cry

thought
happy
smile

seed of thought
growth of feeling
fruit of action

I think therefore I am

TICK TOCK

Tick tock goes the clock
seconds

tick tock goes the clock
minutes

tick tock goes the clock
hours

tick tock goes the clock
days

tick tock goes the clock
months

tick tock goes the clock
years

tick tock the clock stops
6 feet under ocean docks

tick tock goes the clock
never stops
new beginning starts

JOYFUL MUSIC TEARDROPS

Joyful music teardrops
deepen cracks
in earth depression

sunflower seeds sprout
from depression cracks
touching sun rays

save me save me
I'm sinking into depression

let me ride sunflower shoots
back to sun rays

crying to
joyful music teardrops

INNOCENT LOST

Laughter rings
room sings
girlish notes
echo puberty

birthday dreams
sweet sixteen
virgin screams
lost virginity

laughter dies
room cries
girlish moans
echo innocence gone

I AM A ???

I am a ???

I am a seed
I am a root
I am a trunk
I am a branch
I am a bud
I am a flower
I am a fruit

I am a ???

SCHERZANDO

Ravens lustful song
draws me seductively
into self destruction
blind eyes wide shut

doves love song
draws me scherzando
into self building
seeing eye narrow open

raven verses dove
spiritually battling
ultimate prize
my Soul

SOME WHERE IN THE WORLD

Some where in the world

my breath is in time with
some ones last breath at death
some ones first breath at birth

some where in the world

my tear is in time with
some ones tear of pain at death
some ones tear of joy at birth

some where in the world

my heart beat is in time with
some ones last heart beat at death
some ones first heart beat at birth

A SINGLE TEAR

A single tear

dropped from my eye
i died
of dehydration

a single tear

dropped from your eye
i revived
of hydration

father forgive them
for they know not
what they do

FOR WHOM THE BELL TOLLS

Free will free will
bridging decision's mill
do what is right
engage in life's fight

hurry up and wait
for destinies fate
dreams you create
before it's too late

a life of heaven
a life of hell
ringing within your soul
for whom the bell tolls

it tolls for thee

LUMINESCENCE MOTHS

A drop of your sunshine
entered my dark soul
bringing to light
deeds done in secret

i enjoy my deeds
fulfilling my selfish needs
you torture me
with your sharing love plea

my dark soul warms
melting like chocolate
savored by hungry swarms
of luminescence moths

B. E. A. S. T.

Bacchanalia
Emasculate
Afreet
Sadomasochism
Tabes dorsalis

i starved the beast
it wouldn't die
growing like a weed
in my soul's garden

i fed the beast
it died of gluttony
decaying like a flower
in my soul's garden

KNOCK KNOCK

Knock knock
who's there
God

God who?
I don't know you

knock knock
who's there
Jesus

Jesus who?
I don't know you

knock knock
who's there
Holy Spirit

Holy Spirit who?
I don't know you

knock knock
who's there
satan

Satan who?
Oh, i know you

come in come in
to my den of sin
my beloved friend

FLAMING MOTH

My dark side
disgust me
I'm drawn to it
like a moth to the flame

cold flames
freeze my soul
soften me
like a rock

rocks stuck in motion
spinning in stillness
destroying myself
music to others

music like lily pads
wraps around
my oak tree trunk
choking me

lily pads
blanket the

mosquito infested
pond of my soul

pond dew drops
evaporate under
sunny moon
i die of thirst

moon reflects
optical illusions
of myself
blindly seeing

seeing i want to die
instead i blindly cry
living in death's hell
dying under heaven's spell

DARKNESS BROKE

A young seed breaks
through the darkness
of mother's egg

trying to touch the
Sun

a young baby breaks
through the darkness
of mother's womb

trying to touch the
Sun

a young son breaks
through the darkness
of mother's children

trying to touch the
Sun

The Light
replaces
The Sun

JUDAS KISS

I am remembered
by my worst mistake
u are remembered
by hanging on a stake

i betrayed u
with a kiss
u betrayed me
with forgiveness

Father Forgive Them
For They Know Not
What They Do

ENCOUNTER

You blanket me like snow
covering me inch by inch
hiding all the dirt and trash
littered on my ugly heart landscape

I'm so beautiful to look at
covered in your white snowflakes
i try to forget I'm ugly
disguised by your pretty makeup

why do you love me?
Falsely presenting me
as a pretty snow angel
just to make others smile

the sun comes out
rising degree by degree
revealing my dirt and trash
I cry out to you

You see me
for who i am
and lovingly say:

I Will Never Leave You
Nor Forsake You

LOVE TRIANGLE

You handed me the forbidden fruit
tempting me with lustful ill repute
i ate it like a love struck fool
breaking god's one and only rule

i saw you were nude
i had naughty thoughts so lewd
i then felt guilt and shame
my life no longer the same

our new found knowledge
forced us to acknowledge
banishment from the garden
meant death with no pardon

You heard our repentant cries
changed our suffering lives
died for all our sins
pardoned us so we can live again

CHICKEN LITTLE

The sky is falling
death is calling

trouble events descend
thundering me like a rainy friend
i only get a moment of sun
until trouble events put me in a panicky run

the sky is falling
death is calling

my car brakes fail
shooting me like a rocket hail
i barely stop in time
almost slamming into another's behind

the sky is falling
death is calling

i receive a call on the cell phone
caller id says it's you with an audible bleep

it's not you but your sons voice speaking sadly monotone
telling me you had died in your sleep

the sky is falling
death is calling

TANGLED WEB

It was a warm day in spring
i should have been with my men at war
i send another to command instead therefore
going in the evening to my sunroof to view a plaything

i spied on you from my high sunroof
watching you bath nude and aloof
your beautiful body had me entranced
i plotted to touch you intently was my stance

i sent someone to find out who you were
i was told you were a married women and spoken for
your husband was fighting in the war
i sent for you to come see me like a saboteur

when the cats away
the mice will play
i seduced you taking you to my bed to lay
you conceived exposing me like an x-ray

oh what a tangled web we weave
when first we practice to deceive
i killed your husband to hid the crime
the baby died during the wintertime

REBEL HEART

I was the first ever born
filled from the start with hate and scorn
you were my younger brother
given birth by our tempting mother

i was a bad farmer
wanted to be a snake charmer
you were a good shepherd
your sheep beautiful and peppered

i made an offering of stale corn
it was despised like the world of porn
you made an offering of fatty meat
bringing delight like a winning lottery receipt

i grew angry and hated you for being good
i thought to kill you with a piece of wood
i invited you out to my yellow cornfield
attacking you and raging that you would never heal

you cried out to me with a merciful appeal
i laughed watching your bloody body beginning to congeal

i watched a crow bury it's young in the sacred ground
i did the same to you so you would never be found

your blood cried from the red sticky ground
making noises like a squeaky old merry go-round
i knew then that it was only a matter of time
before everyone would know of my sadistic crime

i was asked where is thy brother
i felt like i was about to smother
i said i know not: am i my brother's keeper
i then saw the face of a laughing grim reaper

i cried out that i didn't want to also die
even though i was a angry terrible guy
you had mercy and instead gave me a mark
i will now forever wander like a great white shark

SILENT SCREAMS

Opposing thoughts in my dreams play ping pong
creating as they bounce over the net vivid pictures of right and wrong
one leads to movies of you wearing a black thong
one leads to movies of you singing a swan's birdsong

inside my bipolar mind i silently scream
tossed back and forth like a stormy tide midstream
controlled by nature's force of a full moonbeam
i try not too but end up having a wet dream

i wake up feeling guilty and ashamed
crying out fears wanting to be unchained
wishing for my dirty dreams to be tamed
with no opposing thoughts and instead a victor proclaimed

SNAKE MAIDEN

You slithered into the dance club wearing a short red revealing dress of
Seduction
your glassy snake eyes leering for potential unknowing victims of
abduction
your dripping body sweat from dancing transmitted a heated electrical
conduction
turning the now slimy wet dance floor into an orgy of teasing
swimming
construction

men bought you drinks in exchange for groping dances making a
wallet
deduction
becoming drunken by your gyrating hips of demonic dancing
Seduction
you handily led them to erectly drown in lustful fiery
destruction
becoming your scaly robots unable to seemingly
function

they became your loyal students in your school of sexual
induction
listening to your life's sensual tricks of
instruction
your spilt tongue game of lewd
Seduction
created in them a high wall of good moral
obstruction

they became obedient actors in your sadistic earthly
production
populating the world so there would never be a satanic
reduction
filling their minds with subversive thoughts of heavenly
deconstruction
their only mission in life now is to spawn future snake babies of
Seduction

FETTLE ROSE PETAL

My truck has 4 tall wide monster tires
one was squeaking badly which requires
me to give it all my temporary focused attention
while the 3 good tires caused me no apprehension

same thing applies to the greedy bias news media
bad news constantly broadcast for high rating expedia
making the world seem almost always bad
making me anxious mad and sad

i believe for every 1 tragic bad event
3 inspiring good events are happening in the present
i rarely see any good events on the greedy bias news
i think it's their way to keep up in a constant state of the blues

wake up and smell the roses
don't stay focused on the thorn that opposes
see the beauty in the red healing petal
and focus on the health benefits of the roses aroma fettle

FREEWILL VERSES RULES

You made the 10 golden rules
to obey them i get a reward of eternal jewels
i daily with intention break them
fleeing to the fiery lake for a birthday swim

if you had not made the 10 golden rules
i wouldn't be laden down like a pack mule
i wouldn't always be in constant trouble
like the optical lens of the space telescope Hubble

i like popping life's status quo soap bubble
overtime turning buildings into concrete rubble
you try to keep me confined in a round bottle cage
like red wine that gets better with age

i like dangerous extremes
i want to live out my dreams
you try to keep things in balance
dying to show off my three nailed talents

you are of a heavenly mind
forgiving me that i am blind
i am of a earthly mind
just want to have fun and unwind

SHEEPISH WOLF

I watched you on TV.
Trying to serve two masters

your first word is your love of God
your second word is your love of money
your lips drip of Luke warm honey
your message is hypocritically funny

we all know that oil and water don't mix
though you attempt to with your stirring spoon tricks
your true goal is to line your pockets with silver and gold
falsely pretending to build the Lord's kingdom to save a soul

i read the bible everyday
truth planted in my heart to stay
you may fool others with your spilt tongue double talk
but i listen to the Holy Spirit to teach me how to walk

"No one can serve two masters. Either you will hate the one and love
the other, or you will be devoted to the one and despise the other.
You cannot serve both God and money.

VALENTINE DANCE FEVER

I watched your heart card movements from afar
wishing you would notice me like a flaming star
i watched you take off your red pumps in the park
running and dancing bare foot causing my blood to spark

the dog in me sniffed the breeze smelling your strawberry scent
you smelled also of a chocolate musk that must be heaven sent
i continued to watch you lovingly twirling in the short green grass
you were enjoying the moment and i hoped to make you mine at last

i slowly approached you and ask to join in your love dance
looking in my blue eyes you gave me a white toothy smile
grasping my sweating hand and in a provocative stance
agreed to be my Valentine's day red rosy flower child

ADDICTION

Always
    thinking
        about
            my
                next
                    fix

Dying
    to
   feel
      the
         short
            temporary
                pleasure
                    brought
                        on
                          by
                          the
                            fix

Doing
      whatever
            it
                  takes
                        to
                              fulfill
                                    my
                                          urges

Intense
      feelings
            that
                  i
                        can't
                              control
                                    my
                                          urges

Crying
      with
            shame
                  and
                        guilt
                              after
                                    it's
                                          over
                                                and
                                                      done
                                                            with

Telling
       myself
              afterwards
                     i
                         can
                             quit
                                 and
                                     it's
                                          done
                                              with

Into
     my
          own
              delusional
                     little
                            world
                                 of
                                     pleasure

Only
     using
          others
                   to
                     fullfil
                            my
                                 selfish
                                     pleasure

Never
    admitting
        to
          others
            I
              NEED
                HELP
                  NEED
                    HELP
                      HELP!!!

TWISTED MIND

One foot stands in the dark ocean
one foot stands on the sunny beach
straddled between two opposing worlds
tempted by the rip tide to enter

life is on the sunny beach
death is in the dark ocean
the mind-set of the flesh is death
the mind-set of the Spirit is life

KING RAT

Why do u use me
   like a puppet on a money string
   giving me small bits of **FOOD**
         so i will do their work
why do u use me
   like a puppet on a money string
   giving me small sips of **WATER**
         so i will do their work
why do u use me
   like a puppet on a money string
   giving me minimum **SHELTER**
         so i will do their work
why do u use me
   like a puppet on a money string
   giving your top 1% **EVERYTIIING**
         so i will do their work

AQUA MARINE WOLF PEEK

I watched you from a distance like a hungry wolf
at the Barnes and Noble bookstore
I had watched you on two separate visits
but was never hungry enough to attack you

I was starving to death and decided that today
today I would stalk you and eat you as my prey
you were dressed in soft tan cow hide leather
revealing underneath aquamarine gold tipped pages

I slowly parted and tasted your aqua marine pages
and guiltily read your dying words of wisdom
but I tell you, everyone who looks at a woman
to lust for her has already committed Adultery

with her in his HEART

CAN'T WIN FOR LOSE

I'm thinking of finally letting you go
u are costing me to much dough
every month it never ever fails
I'm increasing someone else's gross sales

I'm caught between a hard place and a rock
unable to afford to let you go and get a better stock
I've paid so much fixing you monthly over the years
to sell you at a loss would cause me to shed much greedy tears

KHARGA OASIS

We grew up in the concrete jungles
you grew up in the sandy glass oasis
we were taught to grow green back bundles
you were taught to serve smiling faces

we travelled 40 days to buy your waterfall oasis
we arrived parched and blistered with smiling faces
you served us ice cream and clear ice cold water
you denied our offer to pay like a Mother Teresa martyr

you invited us to enter your secret Hibis temple
we saw the tan mud brick building that was beautiful and simple
we opened the door and stepped into a golden spiritual school
you told us here our green back bundles would never rule

ODE TO ARTISTIC ALISON

Njeri penned the poem "before the last tear drop"
i e-mailed it to you my artistic daughter before my last tear drop
the poem reminded me so much of the creative you
a beautiful 7 year old painting a heart of love so true

now you are a pretty college woman of 19
seriously thinking of a Studio Art Major Scene
i wish you well in whatever path you chose
supporting you always like a wick in a shining candle you reuse

SMILING DOG

I just walked 3 miles today at the cancer garden park
u walked by me with your brown dog who gave me a good morning
bark
I thought about your brown dog who lives only in the present
u wagged your swishing tail at me giving me a toothy gift smile as a
present

I sat down on the cool metal green park bench
u warmed me up with your shining morning ray
I watched others walk by and was as still as a golden finch
u saw me and happily smiled saying have a good day

I think about the oil change appointment I have at 11
u enter my thinking so I leave a voice mail at 9:07
I think of you and send you a text about the smiling dog
u text back for me to think like the smiling dog

in the clear present moment
not in the cloudy future moment
of the unknown grey distance fog
live the life of a smiling dog

BROKEN BOX ???

We decided you were a broken box
we decided to fix you secured with locks
we got out all our theological carpenters tools
we hammered you to conform to our golden rules

I'm not broken and understand who I am
I changed my name at 18 to Samantha from Sam
I have always been bullied and picked on in school
I am true to myself and pry out your nailing rules

we see you as a lost broken box
I see myself as a found music jukebox
we see you through the eyes of eastern orthodox
I see myself through the eyes of life's hard knocks

I just want to be accepted for who I am
I hate being judged and told I am a scam
I was born this unique special way
I am aware of what your beliefs say

Matthew 7

1 "Do not judge, or you too will be judged. 2 For in the same way you judge others, you will be judged, and with the measure you use, it will be measured to you.

3 "Why do you look at the speck of sawdust in your brother's eye and pay no attention to the plank in your own eye? 4 How can you say to your brother, 'Let me take the speck out of your eye,' when all the time there is a plank in your own eye? 5 You hypocrite, first take the plank out of your own eye, and then you will see clearly to remove the speck from your brother's eye.

I don't judge you
please don't judge me
I'm only a broken box
in your eyes can't you see

BIPOLAR GOD ???

God said an eye for an eye
    said turn the other cheek

God said kill your enemies
    said love your enemies

God in the old testament
    in the new testament

God are you BIPOLAR ?
          LIKE
          ME

ELEPHANT DONKEY BIRTH

Elephant
make America great again
donkey
make America whole again

elephant
build a wall
donkey
tear down walls

elephant
tax cuts for the rich
donkey
tax cuts for the poor

elephant
minimum wage increase is bad
donkey
minimum wage increase is good

elephant
ride the elephant and feel tall
ride the donkey and feel small

donkey
ride the donkey and feel brave
ride the elephant and feel slaved

3D TWISTER

Desire
I AM

        sky turned spinning black
        saw your twirling destructive back
        fell down on my scared sinful knees
        asked God "save me please"

Discern
I AM

        heard a loud rumbling fiery black train
        time slowed down in my trembling brain
        splintered wood cross nailed my repentant screams
        asked God "save me from these hellish demon things"

Do
I AM

        opened my streaming tear shut born again eyes
        sun was shining brightly to my awestruck surprise
        white cotton ball clouds in the sky now heavenly blue
        asked God " save me eternally so I AM a witness for you"

SMALL ELEPHANT HANDS TRUMPED

4 elephants debated in a red grassy field
trying to trump each other with their handy will
mouth and lips fingering where each one stands
little Marco elephant trumps Donald elephant has small hands

Donald elephant raised his big thick stiff hard long trunk in alarm
bearing his two bloody sharp tusks looking extremely strong
his large ears turned a fiery cherry blossom red
and this is what Donald elephant shouting said

little Marco elephant made fun of my hands
nobody has ever hit my hands
look at my hands
are those small hands?

Little Marco elephant said that if my hands are small
something else must be small
I guarantee
there's no problem

BLIND RAINBOW FISH

Rainbow fish swimming unaware
in the reef with red shark eyes that stare
rainbow fish nibble on morsels of food
unaware orange sharks are on the death move

rainbow fish are taken by complete surprise
deceived by the predatory yellow sharks deceptive lies
rainbow fish are cornered with no where to turn
eaten by the green sharks who make the ocean churn

rainbow fish think they are safe in large numbers
only to be singled out by blue sharks who never slumber
rainbow fish are blind to their unfortunate fate
eaten by indigo and violet sharks into the evening late

DAD'S 3 SHADOWS

Saturday sunshine beams on trinity me
3 shadows on mother earth are blackly cast
single parent of 2 makes sun shadows 3
3 shadows aged 52, 19, 18 at once is a eclipse blast

I'm dads own shadow at senior adult 52
I'm at Amherst McDonalds watching CNN
trump is speaking saying his words are true
asking for my vote and to be his friend

I'm dads daughter shadow at young women 19
I'm in Fredericksburg buying a car with my boyfriend
we're driving allot of miles watching the highway 29 scene
it will be nice to drive a car not always on the mend

I'm dads son shadow at young man 18
I'm in Rustburg at the home of my girlfriend
we're watching shows with a romantic comedy theme
it will be 3 years together with love that will never end

SUNNY BRIAR LAKE

Red headed woodpecker tapped Morse code
on dark dead oak tree where worms abode
2 sweet Briar students with their brown dog walked by
turning around on the metal green bench we all said hi

watched 3 geese swim around a drowned tree in the lake
its twisted limbs protruding out of the water like a desperate snake
wind ripples the water sending a cool breeze off the lake
put on my green stocking hat and began to shake

looking up at the huge white clouds in the sky so blue
my mind day dreams of heaven and I think of you
you gave up your young 33 year old life so I could live
fish jumps out of the water reminding me you said forgive

PERVERSE PLEASURE

My God, My God, why have You forsaken me?
Deliver me from these people who laughingly torture me, don't you
see?
They stripped me naked and drew my blood with their entertainment
whip
my once healthy body becomes torn and shredded into meat strips

My God, I cry by day, but You do not answer me
he smiles as he pierces my side with a long sharp spear
causing the blood thirsty watching crowd to began to cheer
my lungs fill with blood and water as I drown in a spectator ocean sea

you made me charge you once more with your whishing red flag
I fell to my weaken bloody knees which began to slowly drag
dying crying bull speaks to the majority crowd causing them to an-
grily boo
bulls last words are "Father, forgive them for they know not what they
do"

WOLF SHEPHERD

Jesus the good shepherd brought out all his own sheep
going on ahead of them giving them peaceful sleep
the sheep faithfully follow him
and recognize his soothing voice

they will never follow a wolf shepherd voice
God gave them freewill and a choice
in fact, they will run away from him fast
hearing the wolf in sheepskin temper blast

exposed, now the church numbers dwindle to a few
the wolf shepherd attacks the remaining flock anew
wolf shepherd is a hired hand
mad at the sheep who take a stand

WATER WALKER

I am a stripped bass named Jake
I was looking for food in my lake
I looked up and was surprised to see
two barefoot feet walking above me

I had never seen this in all my years
I must admit I was at first filled with fears
once my thumping heartbeat slowed down
I followed the bare feet to see where they were bound

I watched him approach a wooden boat real slow
the men started to scream "I think it's a ghost, I don't know"
water walker said "don't be afraid, it's me"
"open your blind eyes, can't you see"

one man on the boat was bolder than the rest
he stepped out of the boat to prove he was the crew's best
he stepped onto the water and began to walk as well
I now saw four bare feet as the wavy wind began to yell

I saw the boatmen's bare feet began to sink
I saw his face turning pale then fearfully pink
water walker saved the fisherman as he began to thrash and shout
water walker said " you of little faith, why did you doubt?

HIRED HAND SHEPHERD

Hired hand shepherd preaches to his faithful flock
"turn the other cheek and never stop"
"God needs your money seed
give it to me, I will help others in need"

unpaid shepherd preaches to his faithful flock
"turn the other cheek and never stop"
"God needs your money seed
give it to orphans and widows in need"

hired shepherd reacts to his slapped cheek
"an eye for an eye and a tooth for a tooth"
"I will return your slap back and slap you too
turning your red cheeks black and blue"

unpaid shepherd reacts to his slapped cheek
"turn the other cheek and never stop"
"I will never return your slap back as you slap me too
turning my red cheeks black and blue"

MANIC MOON

Orange sun dawned in my brain
awoke to dark dusk, I began to rain
sleep would abandon me once again
manic moon arrived, my play friend

sleep is who I really miss
manic moon starts envy twist
manic moon wants to play
keeping sleep far away

sleep, please return my friend
manic moon wants me hospitalized again

now I lay me now to sleep
I pray the Lord my soul to keep
if I die before I wake
I pray the Lord my soul to take

VOLCANO TEARS

Hot cherry glowing volcano tears
melted lava rock blacken heart
soft red malleable clay born
reshaped by Potter's hands

heated in life's fiery furnace
hardened and glazed to perfection
communion heart lava cup shared
overflowing with red watery tears

drunken as clear bloody wine

JEALOUS TRUCK

Last month you cost me 175.73 for an alternator
next Wednesday you will cost me 255.00 for a radiator
I know you are jealous of my girlfriend
making me so broke she traded me in for a rich boyfriend

I guess you are happy now that's she is gone
now it's just you and me alone
your jealous ways are getting out of hand
you keep it up and I'll post a "For Sale" sign at a road stand

BREAD FISHING

Fishing was good today
walked to 4 different lakes, no fish got away
no windy ripples in the waters
cast bread as bait for starters

bass ate the bread on the top water
as it sank slowly to the lake bottom
then eaten by bottom feeding catfish
becoming the "Special of the Day" bread dish

the caught fish ate all my bread of tears
consuming it released all their unforgiving fears
now they are swimming happy and glad
in heaven now forgiven and never sad

SUNNY BRASS CLOUD

We wandered on our knees to the mountain high
your face shone like the sun in a cloudless blue sky
your clothes became white as snow reflecting light
two dead men suddenly appeared before our startled sight

we spoke to build three barbed wired shelters that wouldn't fall
a sunny brass cloud emerged brightly overshadowing us all
thunder and lightening voice booms "Listen to Him, He is my Son"

we fell on our scared faces and mutely shakily laid
you gently touched us saying "arise, be not afraid"

we lifted up our frightful eyes and with a open stare
noticed the two dead men had disappeared, no longer there

we wandered on our knees to the mountain low
you told us "say nothing to anyone down below"

we had to wait until you were dead
and rise from the grave to rule instead

now we are able to tell your vision story
to future generations you will raise to immortal glory

O Death, Where is your victory?
O Death, Where is you sting?

EARTHWORM MARATHON RACE

The spring rain gun sounded
wetting the ground with liquid bullets
breast stroking I emerged from mother earths womb
joining thousands of others racing from the tomb

in front of me was a two lane black dessert
wet with liquid bullets allowing me to swim across
in the middle was a yellow divide
to win, I had to reach the other side

I started my stride with thousands of others
all of them were my sisters and brothers
beyond the black dessert was our goal
green land of milk and honey, legends foretold

birds started attacking us from the air
i continued swimming, avoiding their death stare
big black round monsters smashed most again and again
i continued swimming, focusing on my family within

the sun came out as i reached the yellow line
halfway to finishing, i was still swimming fine
the liquid bullets began to disappear
my swimming became labored, i began to fear

blinded by the bright sun, my swimming slowed
the liquid bullets no longer flowed

just as i was about to give up
thinking i would surely burn up
i smelled the green finish line

knowing i would win and be fine
i cross into the green land of milk and honey
"it will be nice having a family where it's always sunny"

VIRGINIA BEACH EYES

Eye watch the waves roll onto the beach
eye don't hear them roar

eye watch you running in the sand
eye don't hear your feet

eye watch you walking your dog on the boardwalk
eye don't hear him bark

eye watch the seagulls flying
eye don't hear them call

eye watch you take pictures of King Neptune
eye don't hear the camera click

eye am?
Virginia Beach Web Cam

NIGHT TEMPTERS

Awaken in
middle of
NIGHT

two voices
in my
HEAD

basic instructions
before leaving
EARTH

deny myself
and follow
YOU

follow the
one who
ROSE

!! SURPRISES

Apple falls
balloon rises
no surprises

sun sets
sun rises
no surprises

son dies
son rises
!! surprises

FATAL KISS

Moment of conception

      fatal kiss reception
      starts your action

      dust you are
      dust you return

      you are gone
      I March On

CHOICES

While you're being ignored
your every action is on record
waiting until you do some wrong
showing the court your will's not strong

you had freewill to chose
behave in public or lose
freedom and be in jail
living in a earthly hell

MUSICAL APPLE

Eve's musical apple
sings alto notes
Adam's bass heart
booms with love

Adam follows his heart
instead of his head
chose eve over God
now he is dead

TIDE MOON DANCE

18 year old James

          dock of bay
          love to stay
          beach beckons me

sand was hot
sand now cold
moon dances tide

tide rolls in
tide rolls out
What's life about?

52 year old James

          dock of bay
          love to stay
          beach beckons me

sand was cold
sand now hot
tide dances moon

tide rolls out
tide rolls in
Love's life about!

POEM SEED

Blank mind
wasting time
poem seed
ink me

watch grow
under snow
green sprout
now out

mature seed
fruit yawl
new seed
ink me

SURPRISE KISS

Hidden in wait
behind the door
to kiss me

with immortality
of surprise
in eyes

PATTY PINCHED

My name is patty
I'm plump and fatty
forgot to wear green
leprechauns pinched me extreme

SPRING RAIN

You wept down slow
causing flowers to vastly grow
seeping into mother earth fast
causing green grass to grow at last

grass is nitrogen feed
mower taken from shed

your wind made breaking twigs
causing nest building rigs
birds drink your love dew treats
causing new little heart beats

old man winters on a run
causing Spring Rain to return

TREE BREATH

I breathe in life
i breathe out death

my breath of life
        is
your breath of death

my breath of death
        is
your breath of life

i live because of you
you live because of me

life and death intertwined

life of tree
life of man

defined:

"We both must Live to Survive"

EYES HAIKU

Our eyes briefly met
i shyly looked far away
in Love at first sight

DECK OF CARDS HAIKU

All cards from deck dealt
past day, today, future day
Death holds winning hand

BREAST LOVER HAIKU

I am a breast man
Wendy's finger licking good
marathon chicken

BREAST FED HAIKU

Spring nourishes all
in land of milk and honey
bees change diapers

CABBAGE PATCH BABY HAIKU

Female sends e-mail
to male stork to deliver
cabbage patch baby

TEARY KISS HAIKUS

She kissed me gently
her tears took my breath away
you lived as i died

she kissed me gently
her tears took my breath away
you died as i lived

SUN ROSY HAIKU

Morning sun rosy
rising in blooming garden
painting white clouds red

WANDERING SHEEP HAIKUS CHAPTER 1

A young sheep among
a flock wandered, and as he
looked around he said

"the grass is greener
over there, i'll go yonder
and not have to share"

looking and thinking
the shepherd was turned away
the young sheep bolted

and ran toward the
field far, far away
as he ran he thought

"I'm Free!" I'm Free!" "Free!"

WANDERING SHEEP HAIKUS CHAPTER 2

Upon reaching the
field of green grass, the young sheep
began to eat fast

with unseeing eyes
didn't notice a wolf pack
ascend over rise

as the pack wolves ran
drawing nearer to their prey
the young sheep looked up

seeing them he ran
frantically looking for flock
seeing none caused shock

WANDERING SHEEP HAIKUS CHAPTER 3

Running and looking
the young sheep entered the woods
and started shouting

"I'll run in the woods,
I'll get away from the wolves
before it's too late"

without second thoughts
the young sheep entered; not find
the safety he sought

the light grew from bright
to dim; he could barely see
in front of himself

WANDERING SHEEP HAIKUS CHAPTER 4

Deeper in the woods
he was engulfed in a fog;
stumbled into bog

finally he stopped;
young sheep not realizing
he was in quicksand

listening for the wolves
he heard them distantly howl;
they seemingly growled

"Oh foolish sheep who's
wandered astray, the vast bog
will eat you today"

WANDERING SHEEP HAIKUS CHAPTER 5

Chills ran down his spine
as the young sheep tried to run
to make up lost time

but he could not move
the quicksand held him steadfast;
sunk, quick breathe was last

sheep heard wolves laughing;
not even feeling the crook
of the Shepherd's staff

hooked around his neck,
Shepherd pulls sheep from sand's death
saved my selfish life

LIFE'S COLOR PALETTE HAIKU

Happy is yellow
sad is the color of blue
mixing births life green

PEEK-A-BOO KITTY

Peek-A-Boo

i see you
hide in hole

i baited
i watched
i waited

you did show
my hunger fed
my hunger dead
you in bed

NET FISHING

I cast my net upon the sea
"im so hungry, let me catch fish"
was my plea

i drew my net from the sea
100 fish were in the net
1 got away with a flip-flop step

i dove in the ocean
i caught you at last
100 eaten at fish fry blast

BRUSSELS ATTACK HAIKU

I, american
sorry for your loss of lives
today, i CRY too

SPRING SEEDS PLANTED

                     fall fruit
          in spring
seeds planted

                  pain action
         grows
pain thought

                  hurt action
         grows
hurt thought

                  anger action
         grows
anger thought

                  hate action
         grows
hate thought

revenge action
grows
revenge thought

kill action
grows
kill thought

love action
grows
love thought

YOU HIDE I SEEK

I count to 100
game begins

u hid in tree
still in crack

u part leaves
see me

i see u
fun begins

u trip
expose all

i tag
u it

game over
play again

NO MEANS YES KINESICS HAIKU

You tell me oh no
your body language says yes
i sell you a car

NEAPOLITAN TREAT HAIKU

I smell vanilla
i touch strawberry, feels good
i eat chocolate

MARCH KITE DISPLAY

Windy kites lifting
colorful tails on display
i love windy days

SUN PEEKS SNOWFLAKES HAIKU

Sun peeked through your clouds
exposing your white snowflakes
i grew warm inside

YADA YADA YADA HAIKU

You've talked for two hours
stopping only between breaths
she nods, stops listening

WHITE HONEY FLOWER HAIKU

Trees are now blooming
honeybees drink white flowers
produce nature's sweets

SPILL THE BEANS HAIKU

Today beans were spilled
beauty and beast election
chose Trump or Cruz wife

VIRGINIA BEACH SEAGULLS HAIKU

I saw you today
on virginia beach webcam
king neptune feeds you

SHADOW WALKING HAIKU

I am sun flying
casting shadows on your walk
sands of time march on

KING NEPTUNE HAIKU

I stand over you
guard you as you worship me
i am King Neptune

EASTER EGG HUNT

J ames awoke sunday
E very easter always
S urrounded by a basket
U nder his bed of a
S weet milk chocolate bunny and eggs

E ggs of different sizes and
M any colors such as blue, green and
E ven one big prize
R ed egg representing the blood of Christ
G iven as a sacrifice and
E ven cracking the prize red egg
S ymbolized his resurrection from the dead

F rom out of his room james
R an to his mom all excited
O nly to see instead a giant bunny and many friends.
M otioning for them to all stay inside and

T elling them to wait until told and
O nly then could they run outside and find the
M any hidden eggs, especially the big red prize egg with the
B unny rabbit which springs out alive

FROG BREATH HAIKU

Princess hates kissing
the prince who always has bad
lily pad frog breath

TWISTED MIND HAIKU

One foot in the sea
tempted by the rip tide to
leave beach; dive in wave

EASTER DISCIPLE HAIKU

Deny yourself and
take up your cross and follow
me my disciple

BOOK SMILE HAIKU

You accepted book
breaking out into big smile
enjoy it my friend

FREE CHICK-FIL-A COUPON HAIKU

Free chicken sandwich
from stranger; paid it forward,
gave to another

ONE, TWO BUCKLE MY SHOE HAIKUS

One, two buckle shoe
three, four close the past back door
five, six pick up steps

seven, eight walk straight
nine, ten present day begins
live like your last day

ALISON TREY QUESTION HAIKUS

What is the best thing
i have ever done in life?
you replied, "Have Us"

love you Alison
best thing i have ever done!
love you Trey, my son

CLOUDY SUN SUNNY CLOUD HAIKUS

Cloudy this morning
walking and now it's sunny
mind of bipolar

clouds bring me so low
sun puts me in manic high
weather changes me

BEACH RETIREMENT HAIKU

Life's not on the beach
life's with family and friends
retire to them now

TORCH RACE HAIKU

You are at start line
i am near the finish line
i hand you the torch

NEVER MIND HAIKU

You text me with words
not fast enough of reply
you text "Never Mind"

LOVERS WEDDING PLAN HAIKU

I type as you speak
"i toss, you remove garter"
"toast, open dance floor"

CHILDREN'S RAINBOW

Sprinklers start running
two children began to shout
"mom, it's a rainbow

JUDGED BOOK BY COVER HAIKU

Cup set by trash can
waitress put cup in trashcan
"lazy grey haired man"

FACEBOOK HAIKU

Made a facebook page
see my family and friends
very happy now

WHEELCHAIR HAIKU

Brought in a wheelchair
can not move, can only stare
take care my dear friend

WALKING MOMENTS HAIKU

The moment of life
steps with the moment of death
walk in that moment

NATURES LULLABY HAIKU

There's peace in silence
natures lullaby to me
allows peace within

EYE WITNESS CAM HAIKU

I'm a human cam
writing haiku poems of my
eyewitness events

INKED HAIKU

You raised up your shirt
showing me your new tattoo
i showed you mine too

TRASHY PINE NEEDLES

Many years of pine needles
infested with black beetles
built up on the side of the road
each year becoming a heavier load

cigarette butts were in the pine mix
discarded by addicts getting their cancer fix
pieces of plastic were also there
thrown by others who don't care

a dove spotted the trash from above
used it to build a nest of love
year after year the dove removed pieces of the load
turning it into bigger nests for others to abode

a labor of love by the dove
removing my trash day by day
forgiving me of my trashy ways
leaving behind a heart image of agape love

FORGOTTEN PERFUME KISS

I was taking a walk
passing strangers along the way
living in the present moment
mind far away

you saw me from a distance
i never saw you
you always like to surprise me
you blew me a kiss

like cupid with his arrow
you hit me in the heart
i stopped in my tracks
your breezy kiss entered my nose

i slowly turned around
your perfume still in the air
you had returned back to me
spring just cut green grass

KEG BELLY HAIKU

Gambrinous drunk
opened another large keg
full of beer with friends

ALISON'S GIGGLE SONG

You missed me today
i was working far away
your eyes filled with tears
you felt i had been gone for years

your mom didn't know what to do
your crying was making her blue
she called me on the phone
her voice in a upset tone

i said everything will be fine
put daddy's girl on the line
she held the phone to your ear
i began to sing to you with cheer

"alison, alison
you're so pretty alison
you're so pretty
you're so smart
daddy loves you
from his heart"

your crying stopped and fled
turning to giggles instead
not even a single tear
daddy's voice was here

i sung your song this morning my star
riding with you in your red car
it still makes you laugh and giggle
my 19 year old artist who use to squiggle

WALNUT JONES SNOW
VELOCITY COLUMNS

W hite
A nimal
L arge
N ose
U ndressed
T oes

J umps
O n
N early
E veryones
S hoes

S mells
N ature
O bviously
W ild

V ery
E nergetic
L oves
O thers
C unny
I ntellect
T eeth
Y oung

C an
O nly
L eap
U nder
M asters
N OW
S IC

STEPHANIE'S BIRTHDAY HAIKU

Stephanie's Birthday
she's no april fool, she is
very, very Cool

OAK LEAF SONG HAIKU

marcescence oak trees
sing psithurism "Auld Lang Syne"
January starts

POISON IVY VINE

You and i
sprouted together

two opposing personalities
intertwined

opposites attract so
we intermingled

side by side
growing forever

until you
killed me

with your
....

HAYLOFT PARADISE STADIUM

Rain drives me into dry barn
composing love songs on tin roof
i was thinking of only you
conflicted feelings of what i had done

you had asked me to beat you
you had never felt pain
i reluctantly complied
then eagerly obliged

i sat in hayloft thinking "what have i done"
you came in from soaking rain
i told you "i'm sorry", laying my head on your chest
your heart beating fast through your wet white dress

we rounded 1st base
almost stopped at 2nd base
picked up speed rounding 3rd base
sliding pleasantly fulfilled at the Home plate

scoring a winning run in
Hayloft Paradise Stadium

BROOKS TWINS HAIKU

We met when you're ten
now you are handsome grown men
Happy Birthday Twins

1% KENTUCKY FRIED CHICKEN

1% billionaire chicken rooster
battles
1% millionaire chicken hen

seeing who will rule over
100% clucking chickens

99% clucking chickens have a say
1% clucking chickens rule the day

colonel saunders new recipe plan
99% young chickens take a stand

it's finger licken good
www.kfc.com

PONY TAILED FILLY

She sat relaxed there
blonde hair in ponytail
in her world of make believe

stud was busy neighing
saying truths of deceit
innocence filly listened attentively
not seeing a stud but a stallion

she tithed him her 10%
taking it from the lord
stud used it to buy
red f-150 ford

fix or repair daily
she prayed for forgiveness
stud gave her lust wink
with a sly "i got you" grin

MARCH SMILEY FACE WINDS

felt
   rising roaring ringing hair

saw
   swirling soaring singing eyes

hear
   whistling whirling watering ears

smell
   cooling capering crying nose

taste
   twisting twirling tying mouth

came in like lion
            went out like lamb

BURNING THE MIDNIGHT
OIL MURDER CASE

Clue #1
born 22 may 1859 on Scotland soil
father born on English soil
mother born on Irish soil
educated on Austrian soil

clue #2
father alcoholism caused family turmoil
father psychiatric illness was brain uncoil

clue #3
catholic faith i did recoil
became agnostic spark coil
ending as spiritualist mystic tesla coil

clue #4
doctor treating a boil
no patients to spoil
wrote fiction nights like gargoyle

clue#5
first book caused no reader broil
i still had to work and toil

case solved
Sherlock exposed me like gold foil
royal sir Arthur Conan Doyle

CHILDHOOD BEST FRIENDS
FACEBOOK-UNITED

We grew up together
2 birds of a feather
no memory of meeting you
mind to young for memories to glue

we both were prodigal sons
sowing our wild oats having fun
we parted ways after high school
traveling life's road by our rules

we met Jesus at different times during road bends
He said "Follow me and I will make you fishers of men"
we now go fishing daily where Jesus sends

we crossed paths on www.facebook.com yesterday
after 32 years apart now together again to stay
we both now share Jesus's Love
to others from our hearts of Dove

HANGMAN NOOSE HAIKU

Hangman noose is tied
to the dead tree limb of life
the horse waits for none

BRAXTON DMV BROKEN CAMERA HAIKUS

Pic at dmv
license organ donor made
eye test required

braxton told me to
read first line of what i see
i said was all black

try again she said
i saw first line and i read
passed dmv test

told braxton i was
ugly and broke camera
we both laughed and laughed

ROCKY MOUNTAIN BIGHORN RAM CLASH

The grayish ram and the chocolate ram
were legends among native americans
this is how the story is told
around night fires for generations

grayish ram wandered into
new cooler mountainous region
after feeding on grassy mountain slopes
and alpine meadows

chocolate ram lived in these
rugged rocky cliffs
the bluffs and foothill country
was home

both had pre-orbital glands
at anterior corners of eyes

inguinal glands
in the groin

pedal glands
on each foot

secreting these glands
to support dominance behaviors

both had 30 lb. large horn cores
enlarged corneal
frontal sinuses
bony septa

both weighted a massive
316 lbs.

both grazed on grasses
and shrubs
licking natural salt licks
in the fall and winter

both daily routine was to
eat, rest, ruminate
aiding in effective digestion
and greater body size

both had survived
coyotes, bobcats
lynxes, and golden eagles
when they were young

bears, wolves
and even cougars
tried to kill them and failed
finally leaving them alone

near the rock falls
and falling off cliffs
they saw each other
and locked eyes

both began to display
agonistic behavior
as a winter storm snow began
rapidly building up inch by inch

the two competitors first
walked away from each other
and then turned around
to face each other

jumping and lunging
into head-butts
for a full hour
ignoring the white snowflakes

finally unable to move
through the deep snow
they waited for the sun
eternal friends forever

HOT ROD GARAGE ELECTRIC
CIGAR BOX GUITARS HAIKU

Ron maxey facebook
3 string home made electric
cigar box guitars

COLONEL SAUNDERS 99% CHICKENS FRIED IN WYOMING

Colonel saunders new recipe plan
99% young chickens take a stand

99% young chickens took a stand
colonel saunders won the wyoming land

99% clucking chickens have a say
1% clucking chickens rule the day

1% clucking chickens had their day
1% millionaire hen had her way

GWEN HILL WOODY HAIKU

Friend gwen hill woody
hope you post poems on this site
www.allpoetry.com

WINDY COLD SUN WALK

Walking the cold windy streets
just to feel something inside
no feelings for anyone

you left me yesterday forever
my only life line to emotions
saving me from myself

wind raised chill bumps
felt your cold biting me
awakened me to reality

wind suddenly stopped
felt warmth of your sun
new friend who loves me

WILLOW GREEN LEGENDS

Hi,

i'm willow green
weeping willow tree
grew up in northern hemisphere
400 cousins worldwide

i love interbreeding
creating unique babies
smallest cousins
in artic and alpines

i'm adaptive to mother earth
prefer moist cool conditions
love watching pools, puddles, floods
ponds, streams and lakes

i'm 40ft tall
still growing 10ft a year
starting to beautify landscape
with round drooping branches

i'm a gentle giant
creating shady oasis
pretty green foliage
long thin leaves

my leaves change in fall
turn light green shade
sometimes pretty blue
summertime shade no more

enough of me
want to tell you
legends i've met
in my life time
met ophelia in 1599
broke my willow branch
falling into brook
drowned

met desdemona in 1604
hand on bosom singing
sing willow, willow, willow
sing willow, willow, willow

met stone in 1763
used my milk sap
later felix invented
bayer

met vincent in 1880
used my bark
to write letter
to brother

met rowling in 1971
transplanted me
now guarding
secret garden

met tendulkar in 1989
used my branch
making himself
a bat

met 6 legends so far
you're number 7
look forward
to meeting you

love,
willow green

SHARING LOVE HAIKU

Sharing Love is Back
helping others with problems
please "Pay It Forward"

SOUND OF SILENCE

You left me yesterday
sky not as blue
clouds not as white
sun not as happy

we use to surf the ocean waves
i lay lonely on the glass beach
listening to
sound of silence

hello darkness
my old friend
i've come to
talk with you again

ABOUT THE AUTHOR

James E. Hyler II is a Virginia native who currently resides in the town of Monroe.

He starts each day by feeding the family dog, cat, and birds and going for a 10 mile walk. Hyler is a prolific poet who has had much success publishing his work on www.allpoetry.com under the pen name Sharing Love.

He is the proud father of one daughter and one son and draws strength and inspiration from his faith in Jesus who is Sharing Love in Action and the power of the Holy Spirit who is Sharing Love in Action within us.

He dedicates this book of poems to his daughter, Alison Lynn Hyler, who was born on May 4th, 1996 and will always be an Angel to him.

www.ingramcontent.com/pod-product-compliance
Lightning Source LLC
Chambersburg PA
CBHW072043280526
45788CB00006B/2165